Stewardship
By Jonathan Edwards
Edited by Joel Morris

© 2022 by Joel Morris

Published by: H&E Publishing, Peterbourough, Ontario
www.hesedandemet.com

All rights reserved. This book or any portion thereof may not be reproduced or used in any manner whatsoever without the express written permission of the publisher except for the use of brief quotations in a book review.

Jonathan Edwards, *The Works Jonathan Edwards*, vol. 2 (London: Henry G. Bohn, 1865).

Scripture quotations are from The ESV® Bible (The Holy Bible, English Standard Version®), copyright © 2001 by Crossway, a publishing ministry of Good News Publishers. Used by permission. All rights reserved.

Cover painting: *Thanatopsis* by Asher Brown Durand

Design and layout: Dustin Benge

Paperback ISBN: 978-1-77484-051-1
Ebook ISBN: 978-1-77484-052-8

First edition, 2022

STEWARDSHIP
A Christian Duty

JONATHAN EDWARDS

Edited by Joel Morris

CONTENTS

Biography: The Life and Ministry of Jonathan Edwards		7
Preface		15
1	The Duty	19
2	The Obligation	25
3	The Exhortation	33
4	The Objections	53

"Whoever closes his ear to the cry

of the poor will himself call out

and not be answered."

PROVERBS 21:13

BIOGRAPHY

The Life and Ministry of Jonathan Edwards

Today, Jonathan Edwards (1703–1758) is widely regarded as America's greatest theologian. This was not always so. Sadly, he had been pigeonholed as a "fire and damnation" preacher because of his revival sermon, "Sinners in the Hands of an Angry God." Edwards had been long written off with nothing of value to offer the modern church. In fairness, he did look the part, with his black robes and sharp white collar. It's easy to imagine him thundering from the pulpit and condemning sinners to hell. However, the truth was quite the opposite, as he was softly spoken and thoughtful. Thankfully, in recent decades his great and broad body of work has been rediscovered, with people benefiting all over the world from his beautiful insights and teaching.[1]

Born in 1703, in the wild fringes of the British Empire, Edwards' childhood was spent in East Windsor, Connecticut, in the house of a church pastor. Jonathan's father, Timothy (1668–1759), was a Harvard graduate and pastor in the New England Puritan tradition, which dates back to families who had come over on the *Mayflower*. Timothy was also a revival preacher; childhood experiences must have gone deep in the young mind of Jonathan. He recalls a spiritual awakening as a boy when listening to his father preach.[2]

At 13 years old, he went to study at what is now known as Yale College. His conversion came in 1721, as he read the words of 1 Timothy 1:17. He recounted that he had a new sense of the glory of the divine being, something he'd not experienced before. He sang the words repeatedly to himself and prayed to God that he'd enjoy him, praying for a new affection. This sparked an inward, sweet delight in God and divine things that he would enjoy for the rest of his life. From that time, he understood more of Christ and the work of redemption and glorious work of salvation. The beauty of Christ filled his heart, as his affections and

---

[1] Michael Reeves, *Introducing Major Theologians* (Nottingham: Inter-Varsity Press, 2015), 238–239.

[2] Iain H. Murray, *Jonathan Edwards: A new biography*, (Edinburgh, Banner of Truth Trust, 1987), 3–6.

delight to be religious were rewired to the heart of God.[3]

In 1722, Jonathan cut his study short for his Master's degree once his license for ministry was approved. He was 18 years old when he was called to be a supply preacher in a new congregation in New York City. In pursuit of holiness and gaining valuable ministry experience, Edwards wrote this concerning his time there,

> My sense of divine things seemed to gradually increase, until I went to New York, which was about a year and a half after they began; and while I was there, I felt them, very sensibly, in a much higher degree than I had done before. My longings after God and holiness, were much increased.[4]

His time in New York was brought to an end when the congregation decided to reunify with the parent congregation. Jonathan accepted a call to pastor a church in Bolton. This was short-lived as he eagerly took up a position back at Yale as a tutor in natural science and philosophy, with encouragement from his father and renewed academic interest.[5] It was at Yale that he met Sarah (1710–1758), the daughter of its head founder, James Pierpont (1659–1714).

---

[3] Murray, *Jonathan Edwards*, 35–36.

[4] Murray, *Jonathan Edwards*, 51.

[5] Murray, *Jonathan Edwards*, 52–53.

He married Sarah and would have eleven children with her. In the same year, Jonathan was appointed as assistant pastor to his grandfather Solomon Stoddard (1643–1729). Stoddard was a famous minister in Northampton who died within two years of Edwards arriving. Jonathan succeeded him, and in 1734 through his preaching, revival broke out in Northampton and spread to other towns.

Edwards describes the awakening in 1734 as "the Spirit of God beginning to work extraordinarily and wonderfully." Fueled by his timely preaching on justification by faith, the revival spread and intensified. He saw hundreds come to faith in Jesus. In 6 months, nearly 300 youths started regularly attending his church. By 1735, it had spread perhaps as far as New Jersey. Edwards wrote that "there was worked in them such a holy repose of soul in God through Christ, and a secret disposition to fear and love him, and to hope for blessings from him in this way."[6] However, unexpectedly, a dark phenomenon of a "suicidal craze" overtook scores of unconverted who "hearing voices" were convinced they were doomed for damnation. This is thought to have brought an end to the first wave of revival—spiritual opposition to the move of God among the people. Edwards, the academic, relentlessly documented everything. He wrote *A faithful Narrative of the Surprising*

---

[6] Joseph Tracey, *The Great Awakening* (Edinburgh: The Banner of Truth Trust, 1997), 12–14.

A Christian Duty

Work of God, which inspired other revivals in Britain and America. It significantly impacted Howell Harris (1714–1773) in Wales, who began to pray for another revival.[7]

One might think that the American colonies in 1740 were ripe for this sort of transformation, but this was not so. Religion was on the wane there, despite the previous revival and several local revivals. But God, in his mercy, decided to revisit them. George Whitefield (1714–1770), traveling the thirteen colonies on a revival tour in 1739–1740, visited the colony. Edwards worked with him to organize the tour from Boston to Northampton with Whitefield preaching in Edwards' church. Reminding him of the revival some years before, Edwards wept through the sermon, and the congregation was greatly moved. What a service that must have been! Revival began to spring up again, this time greater than before. This awakening lasted for two whole years and continued longer in other parts.[8] D. Martyn Lloyd-Jones said:

> No man is more relevant to the present condition of Christianity than Jonathan Edwards.... He was a mighty theologian and a great evangelist at the same time.... He was pre-eminently the theologian of revival. If you want to know anything about true revival, Edwards is the man to consult. Revivals have

---

[7] Reeves, *Introducing Major Theologians*, 241.

[8] Murray, *Jonathan Edwards*, 159–160.

often started as the result of people reading volumes as such as these two volumes of Edwards' Works.[9]

Unbelievably, he was dismissed from his pastorate in 1750 after the awakening had subsided; those who resented his theology notably played a part. Edwards' theology was markedly more reformed than that of his grandfather, especially around the sacraments. After being dismissed from the pastorate in 1751, he became a missionary to a tribe of Mohicans at Stockbridge mission station, Massachusetts. Reaching the Indians with the gospel had been a growing passion since perhaps missionary David Brainerd (1718–1747) stayed with the Edwards family to recover his health. Edwards later wrote a biography on his work with the Indians. In 1757, Edwards became President of the College of New Jersey, now known as Princeton College. Shortly after taking office, he died from the smallpox vaccination in 1758.[10]

We have much to learn from the work and life of Jonathan Edwards. He speaks loudly today with things we have not before heard or understood. He was all in for Jesus, with a razor-sharp intellect and unquenchable

---

[9] D. Martyn Lloyd-Jones, *The Puritan Experiment in the New World* (The Westminster Conference Papers, 1976), 103.

[10] Michael A.G. Haykin with Ron Baines, *Jonathan Edwards: A God-centred life, an enduring legacy* (Leominster: Day One Publications, 2013), 5.

passion for God's glory. As a result, God used him as a powerful instrument of renewal for the church. He was a man who was caught up with the beauty of God, a man who delighted in God with the deepest affections. As modern Christians, we seem to have no idea of the riches we can glean from these old saints because they seem dusty and irrelevant. Read him, and you will see he is as relevant today as he was in 1740. Plunge deeply into his works, marvel with him at the glory of God with growing delight in the Lord Jesus!

"Each one must give as he has decided in his heart, not reluctantly or under compulsion, for God loves a cheerful giver."

2 CORINTHIANS 9:7

PREFACE

Joel Morris

Jonathan Edwards knew what it meant to walk in the glorious light of the Kingdom of Heaven, in the day-to-day, here on Earth. It permeated every part of his life, ministry and thought. As a great theologian and thinker of his day, he followed his convictions through to their practical and logical conclusions to application. So, he encouraged Christians to *live a life of holy love here on earth*, to love one another as Christ has loved us. Love that is not in word only, but also in deed. For Edwards', the most natural expression of this love is to help our neighbor and to contribute to their relief. The topic of money is a huge topic in the Bible and also for Christians in Edwards' day. Edwards' writes quite passionately and in detail about our stewardship and charity to the poor, and why it is a duty to be enjoyed for every Christian. He challenges us today as he did his congregation, writing,

> Let everyone examine himself, whether he isn't guilty in this matter. Have you not refrained to give when you have seen your brother in want? Have you not restrained to deny yourselves a little for his relief? Or when you have given, have you not done it grudgingly? And has it not inwardly hurt and grieved you? You have looked upon what you have given, as lost. So that what you have given, has been, as the apostle expresses it, a matter of covetousness, rather than of generosity.[1]

Edwards' theology of stewardship has been greatly overlooked by today's church. The teaching that we are merely stewarding that which the Lord has lent us, is a vital and altogether beautiful discipline. We have bypassed it primarily because we don't understand the spiritual duty expected to be enjoyed by us (especially of generosity to the poor) and have placed some of these teachings in the Old Testament box of stuff we don't know what to do with. We tend to consign these to the ancient nation of Israel from our modern and developed position as nothing to do with today's church whatsoever. Edwards and

---

[1] *The Works of Jonathan Edwards*, vol. 2, (London: Henry G. Bohn, 1865; 10th Edition), 165.

A Christian Duty

his contemporaries certainly didn't view these teachings as we do, because they had a more holistic view of scripture and biblical approach to Christian living. They were being reformed by the gospel in every aspect of life!

I have attempted to gather Edwards' teaching on stewardship into book format drawn from his Miscellaneous Discourses found in the hefty Volume 2 of his works, published in 1865 by Henry G. Bohn. I've taken some liberty to edit and update the language in order to once again make this treasure accessible to today's reader. This is surely a treasure trove that is on display for us through scripture and yet it often slips through our grasp. Edwards makes his case to us today in no uncertain terms as a most important duty to be enjoyed by all. He introduces us to a whole counter-world economy that is revolutionary, as God's economy for his people. I wonder what would happen to our churches, our businesses, our communities and the poor in our world if we Christians practiced this biblical stewardship? I urge you to begin to enjoy this Christian duty with me!

"Give to him freely,

and your heart shall not

be grudging when you give."

DEUTERONOMY 15: 10

ONE

The Duty

The duty enjoined here is giving to the poor. Deuteronomy 15:7 says, "If among you, one of your brothers should become poor, in any of your towns within your land that the Lord your God is giving you, you shall not harden your heart or shut your hand against your poor brother." Here, by "your poor brother," is to be understood the same as in other places as "neighbor." It is explained in Leviticus 25:35, "If your brother becomes poor and cannot maintain himself with you, you shall support him as though he were a stranger and a sojourner, and he shall live with you." "Brother" here is meant not only those of one's own nation, but even "strangers and sojourners."

The Pharisees interpreted it to signify only one of their own nation. But Christ condemns this interpretation in

STEWARDSHIP

Luke 10:29. He teaches, in contradiction to their opinion, that the rules of charity in the law of Moses are to be extended to the Samaritans who were not of their nation and between whom and the Jews there was the most bitter hostility and who were a people very troublesome to the Jews.

God gives us direction in how we are to give in such a case: generously and willingly. We should give generously, and sufficiently for the supply of the poor's need. Deuteronomy 15:7–8 says, "You shall not harden your heart or shut your hand against your poor brother, but you shall open your hand to him and lend him sufficient for his need, whatever it may be." Again, in verse 11, "You shall open wide your hand to your brother, to the needy and to the poor, in your land." We should give willingly and without grudging. Deuteronomy 15:10 states, "And your heart shall not be grudging when you give to him." We may observe how emphatically this duty is emphasized and how much it is insisted on. It is repeated over and over again and emphasized in the strongest terms.

Moreover, God strictly warns against objections. Deuteronomy 15:9 says, "Take care lest there be an unworthy thought in your heart and you say, 'The seventh year, the year of release is near,' and your eye look grudgingly on your poor brother, and you give him nothing, and he cry to the Lord against you, and you be guilty of sin." The matter concerning the seventh year, or year of release, was this: God had given Israel a law, that every seventh year should be a year of release. If any man had lent anything to any of his poor neighbors, if the latter had not been able to repay it before that year, the former should release it and should not exact it of his neighbor but give it to him. Therefore, God warns the children of Israel against making this an objection to helping their poor neighbors. That the year of release was near at hand and it was not likely that they would be able to refund it again before that time, and then they should lose it completely, because then they would be obliged to release it. God foresaw that the wickedness of their hearts would be very ready to make such an objection. But very strictly warns them against it, that they should not be the more backward to supply the wants of the needy for that but should be willing to give him: "You shall be willing to lend, expecting nothing again."

Men have a tendency to make objections against such duties, which God speaks of here as a manifestation of the wickedness of their hearts: "Take care lest there be an unworthy thought in your heart" (Deut. 15:9). The warning is very strict. God doesn't only say, "Take care that you don't actually refuse to give him," but, also take care that you don't have one objecting thought against it arising from a backwardness to generosity. God warns against the beginnings of un-charitableness of the heart and against whatever tends to a reluctance to give. "And you give him nothing, and he cry to the Lord against you, and you be guilty of sin" (Deut. 15:9). God warns them of the guilt which they would be liable to bring upon themselves.

We may observe here several enforcements of this duty. There's a reason implied in God's calling him that is needy, "our *brother*." Deuteronomy 15:9 says, "Take care that your eye look grudgingly on your poor *brother*," and verse 11, "You shall open wide your hand to your *brother*." We are to look upon ourselves as related to all mankind, but especially to those who are of the visible people of God. We are to look upon them as brothers and to treat them accordingly. We shall be low indeed if we be not willing to help *a brother* in want.

Another enforcement of this duty is the promise of God, that for this thing he will bless us in all our works and in all that we put our hands to; a promise that we shall not lose but gain by it (Deut. 15:10). Another is, that we shall never want proper objects of our charity and generosity, "for there will never cease to be poor in the land" (Deut. 15:11). Jesus said in Matthew 26:11, "For you always have the poor with you." This is to cut off any excuse that uncharitable persons would be ready to make for not giving. That they could find nobody to give to, that they saw none who needed. God cuts off such an excuse by telling us that he would so order it in his providence that his people everywhere, in all ages, shall have occasion for the exercise of that virtue.

From this account the doctrine is obvious, that it is the

absolute and indispensable duty of the people of God to give generously and willingly for supplying the wants of the needy. More particularly:

1. It is the duty of the people of God to give generously. It is commanded in the text, "You shall open wide your hand to your brother" (Deut. 15:11). Merely to give something is not sufficient. It doesn't answer the rule, neither comes up to the holy command of God. But we must open our hand wide. What we give, considering our neighbor's wants and our ability, should be such as may be called a generous gift. What is meant in the text by opening the hand wide, with respect to those that are able, is explained in Deuteronomy 15:8, "You shall open your hand to him and lend him sufficient for his need, whatever it may be." By lending here, as is evident by the two following verses, is not only meant lending to receive again, for the word "lend" in Scripture is sometimes used for giving. For example, "Love your enemies, and do good, and lend, expecting nothing in return" (Luke 6:35).

We are commanded to give our poor neighbor what is sufficient for his need. There ought to be none suffered to live in pinching want among the visible people of God, who are able, unless in case of idleness or wastefulness. It is said that the children of Israel should lend to the poor, and in the year of release should release what they had lent, save when there should be no poor among them. It is rendered in the margin, to the end there are no poor among you" (Deut. 15:4). For example, you should so supply the wants of the needy that there may be none among you. This translation seems the more likely to be the true one, because God says that there shall be no such time when there shall be no poor, who shall be proper objects of charity (Deut. 15:11). When people give very sparingly it is no manifestation of charity but of a contrary spirit. As in 2 Corinthians 9:5, "So I thought it necessary to urge the brothers to go on ahead to you and arrange in advance for the gift you have promised, so that it may be ready as a willing gift, not as an exaction."

2. It is the duty of the people of God to give freely. It doesn't answer the rule in the sight of God at all if giving done with an inward grudging, or if the heart is grieved, and it inwardly hurts the person to give. "You shall surely give," says God, "and your heart shall not be grieved." God looks at the heart and the hand is not accepted without it. The Apostle Paul said to the church at Corinth, "Each one must give as he has decided in his heart, not reluctantly or under compulsion, for God loves a cheerful giver" (2 Cor. 9:7).

3. It is the duty of the people of God to be under strict obligation. It is not merely a commendable thing for a man to be kind and generous to the poor, but we are duty bound, as much a duty as it is to pray, or to attend public worship or anything else whatever. And the neglect of it brings great guilt upon any person.

TWO

The Obligation

The duty of giving is absolutely commanded and very much insisted on in the Word of God. Where do we have any command in the Bible laid down in stronger terms and in a more insisting and immediate manner than the command of giving to the poor? We have the same laid down in Leviticus 25:35, "If your brother becomes poor and cannot maintain himself with you, you shall support him as though he were a stranger and a sojourner, and he shall live with you." At the conclusion of Leviticus 25:38, God enforces it with saying, "I am the Lord your God."

Therefore, the duty of giving is mentioned in Scripture, not only as a duty, but a great duty. It is generally acknowledged to be a duty to be kind to the needy. But by many it seems not to be looked upon as a duty of greater importance. However, it is mentioned in Scripture as one of the greater and more essential duties of religion. Micah 6:8 says, "He has told you, O man, what is good; and what does the Lord require of you but to do justice, and to love kindness, and to walk humbly with your God?" Here, to "love kindness" is mentioned as one of the three great things that are the sum of all religion. So, it is mentioned by the Apostle James, as one of the two things wherein pure and undefiled religion consists. James wrote, "Religion that is pure and undefiled before God the Father is this: to visit orphans and widows in their affliction, and to keep oneself unstained from the world" (James 1:27).

In Matthew 23:23, Christ tells us this is one of the weightier matters of the law, "You have neglected the weightier matters of the law: justice and mercy and faithfulness." Again and again, the Scriptures teach us that it is a weightier and more essential thing than the attendance on the outward ordinances of worship. Matthew 9:13 says, "Go and learn what this means: 'I desire mercy, and not sacrifice.'" I know of no duty which is so much insisted, pressed, and urged upon us, both in the Old Testament and New, as this duty of charity to the poor.

This duty of which we are under strong obligation is not only frequently insisted on by God, but it is most reasonable in itself. Therefore, there are two reasons to point out as to why God should insist upon it.

1. It's reasonable considering the general state and nature of mankind. This is such as renders it most reasonable that we should love our neighbor as ourselves, for men are made in the image of our God and on this account are worthy of our love. Besides, we are all nearly allied one to another by nature. We have all the same nature, like faculties, like dispositions, like desires of good, like needs, like aversion to misery, and are made of one blood. We are also made to live by society and union with one another. Mankind, in this respect, are as the members of the natural body, one cannot live alone without a union with and the help of the rest.

This state of mankind shows how reasonable and suitable it is that men should love their neighbors and that we should not look at our own things, but every man also at the things of others (Phil. 2:4). A selfish spirit is very unsuitable to the nature and state of mankind. He who is all for himself and none for his neighbors deserves to be cut off from the benefit of human society. An ungenerous spirit is more suitable for wolves and other beasts of prey than for human beings.

To love our neighbor as ourselves is the sum of the moral law respecting our fellow creatures. To help them and to contribute to their relief is the most natural expression of this love. It is vain to pretend a spirit of love to our neighbors when it is grievous to us to part with anything for their help when under tragedy. They who love only in word and in tongue and not in deed, have no love in truth. Any profession without it is a vain pretense. To refuse to give to the needy is unreasonable because we therein do to others contrary to what we would have others to do to us in the same circumstances. We are very sensitive of our own calamities, and when we suffer, we are more than ready to think that our state requires the compassion and help of others; and ready to think it hard if others will not deny themselves in order to help us when in dire straits.

2. It is especially reasonable considering our circumstances, under such a time of grace as that of the gospel. Consider how much God has done for us, how greatly he has loved us, what he has given us, when we were so unworthy, and when he could have no addition to his happiness by us. Consider that silver and gold, and earthly crowns, were in his esteem but with mean things given to us, he has therefore given us his own Son. Christ loved and pitied us when we were poor, and he poured out himself to help and did even shed his own blood for us without grudging. He did not think much to deny himself and to be at great cost for us vile wretches in order to make us rich, and to clothe us with kingly robes when we were naked. To have us feast at his own table with dainties infinitely costly when we were starving. To advance us from the dunghill and set us among princes and make us to inherit the throne of his glory. To give us the enjoyment of the greatest wealth and plenty to all eternity.

Agreeably to 2 Corinthians 8:9, "For you know the grace of our Lord Jesus Christ, that though he was rich, yet for your sake he became poor, so that you by his poverty might become rich." Considering all these things, what a poor business will it be that those who hope to share in these benefits yet cannot give something for the relief of a poor neighbor without grudging! That it should grieve them to part with a small matter to help a fellow servant in calamity when Christ didn't grudge to shed his own blood for them!

How unsuitable is it for us, who live only by kindness, to be unkind! What would have become of us if Christ had been so saving of his blood and unwilling to bestow it, as many men are of their money or goods? Or if he had been as ready to excuse himself from dying for us, as men commonly are to excuse themselves from charity to their neighbor? If Christ would have made objections of such things as men commonly object to performing deeds of charity to their neighbor, he would have found enough of them.

Besides, Christ, by his redemption has brought us into closer relations one to another, has made us children of God, children in the same family. We are all brothers, having God for our common Father; which is much more than to be brothers in any other family. He's made us all one body. Therefore, we ought to be united and further one another's good, and bear one another's burdens as is the case with the members of the same natural body. If one of the members suffer, all the other members bear the burden with it (1 Cor. 12:26). If one member be diseased or wounded, the other members of the body will minister to it and help it. So surely it should be in the body of Christ.

Apply these things to yourselves. Inquire whether you don't lie under guilt on account of neglect of this duty in withholding that charity which God requires of you towards the needy? You have often been examining yourselves, whether you do not live in some way displeasing to God. Perhaps at such times it never came into your minds, whether you aren't guilty on this account. But this neglect certainly brings guilt upon the soul in the sight of God as is evident by the text. "Take care lest your eye look grudgingly on your poor brother, and you give him nothing, and he cry to the Lord against you, and you be guilty of sin" (Deut. 15:9). This is often mentioned as one of the sins of Judah and Jerusalem for which God was about to bring such terrible judgments. And it was one of the sins of Sodom, for which that city was destroyed, that she did not give to supply the poor and needy.

And haven't we reason to fear that much guilt lies upon this land on this very account? We have a high conceit of ourselves for religion, but don't many other countries shame us? Do not the papists shame us in this respect? So far as I can understand, the tenor of the Christian religion and the rules of the word of God, the same are in no measure in this respect answered by the general practice of most people in this land. There are many who make a high profession of religion. But don't many of them need to be informed by the apostle James, what true religion is?

Let everyone examine himself whether he isn't guilty in this matter. Have you not refrained to give when you have seen your brother in want? Have you not restrained to deny yourselves a little for his relief? Or when you have given, have you not done it grudgingly? And has it not inwardly hurt and grieved you? You have looked upon what you have given, as lost. So that what you have given has been, as the apostle expresses it, a matter of covetousness, rather than of generosity. Have not occasions of giving been unwelcome to you? Have you not been uneasy under them? Have you not felt a considerable backwardness to give? Have you not from a grudging, backward spirit, been quick to raise objections against giving and to excuse yourselves? Such things as these bring guilt upon the soul, and often bring down the curse of God upon the persons in whom these things are found, as we may show more fully hereafter.

"Serve one another,

as good

stewards of God's

varied grace."

1 PETER 4:10

THREE

The Exhortation

We are professors of Christianity; we pretend to be the followers of Jesus and to make the gospel our rule. We have the Bible in our houses. Let us not behave ourselves in this manner: as if we had never seen the Bible, as if we were ignorant of Christianity and knew not what kind of religion it is. What will it signify to pretend to be Christians and at the same time to live in the neglect of those rules of Christianity which are mainly insisted on? But there are several things which I would propose for your consideration:

We Are Stewards

Consider that what you have is not your own, *i.e.,* you have only a subordinate right. Your goods are only lent to you by God, to be improved by you in such ways as he directs. You yourselves are not your own. 1 Corinthians 6:20 says, "You are not your own, for you were bought with a price. So, glorify God in your body." And if you yourselves are not your own, so then neither are your possessions your own. Many of you have by covenant given up yourselves and all you have to God. You have disowned and renounced any right in yourselves or in anything that you have, and have given to God all the absolute right. And if you are true Christians, you have done it from the heart.

Your money and your goods are not your own. They are only committed to you as stewards, to be used for him who committed them to you. 1 Peter 4:9–10 says, "Show hospitality to one another without grumbling. As each has received a gift, use it to serve one another, as good stewards of God's varied grace." A steward has no business to use his master's goods any otherwise than for the benefit of his master and his family, or according to his master's direction. He has no business to use them as if he were the proprietor of them. He has nothing to do with them, only that he is to use them for his master. He is to give every one of his master's family their portion in due season.

But if instead of that, he hoards up his master's goods for himself and withholds them from those of the household, so that some of the family are pinched for hunger and lack of clothing. He is therein guilty of robbing and embezzling from his master. Would any householder put up with such a steward? If he caught him in the act, would he not take his goods out of his hands and commit them to the care of some other steward, who should give every one of his family his portion of meat in due season? Remember that all of us must give account of our stewardship and how we have disposed of those goods which our master has put into our hands. And if when our master comes to reckon with us it be found that we have denied some of his family their proper provision, while we have hoarded up for ourselves as if we had been the proprietors of our master's goods. What account shall we give of this?

Do as to the Lord
God tells us that he shall look upon what is done in charity to our neighbors in want, as done to him; and what is denied them, as also denied him. Proverbs 19:17 states, "Whoever is generous to the poor lends to the Lord, and he will repay him for his deed." God has been pleased to make our needy neighbors his receivers. He in his infinite mercy has so interested himself in their case, that he looks upon what is given in charity to them as given to himself. And when we deny them what their circumstances require of us, he looks upon it as if we rob him of his right.

Christ teaches us that we are to look upon our fellow Christians in this case, as himself, and that our giving or withholding from them, shall be taken, as if we so behaved ourselves towards him (see Matt. 25:40). There Christ says to the righteous on his right hand who had supplied the wants of the needy, "As you did it to one of the least of these my brothers, you did it to me." In like manner he says to the wicked who had not shown mercy to the poor, in verse 45, "As you did not do it to one of the least of these, you did not do it to me." Now what stronger enforcement of this duty can be conceived, or is possible, than this, that Jesus Christ looks upon our kind and generous, or unkind and uncharitable treatment of our needy neighbors as such a treatment of himself?

If Christ himself were upon earth and lived among us in a frail body, as he once did, and were in calamitous and needy circumstances, should we not be willing to help him? Should we be predisposed to excuse ourselves from helping him? Should we not be willing to supply him so that he might live free from distressing poverty? And if we did otherwise, should we not bring great guilt upon ourselves? And might not our conduct justly be very highly resented by God? Christ was once here in a frail body; he stood in need of charity and was maintained by it. He still, in many of his members needs the charity of others.

Necessary and Difficult Duties

Consider that there is an absolute necessity of our complying with the difficult duties of religion. To give to the poor in the manner and measure that the gospel prescribes is a difficult duty, *i.e.* it is very contrary to our corrupt nature, to that covetousness and selfishness of which there is so much in the wicked heart of man. Man is naturally governed only by a principle of self-love. And it is a difficult thing to corrupt nature, for men to deny themselves of their present interest, trusting in God to make it up to them hereafter. But how often has Christ told us of the necessity of doing difficult duties? If we will be his disciples we must sell all, take up our cross daily, deny ourselves, renounce our worldly profits and interests, etc. And if this duty seems hard and difficult to you, don't let that be an objection for you against doing it. For you have taken up quite a wrong notion of things if you expect to go to heaven without performing difficult duties; if you expect any other than to find the way to life on a narrow way.

Love in Deed and Truth

The scripture teaches us that this very particular duty is necessary, particularly,

Firstly, the scripture teaches that God will deal with us as we deal with our fellow creatures and that with what measure we give out to others in this respect, God will measure to us again. This the scripture asserts both ways. It asserts that if we be of a merciful spirit, God will be merciful to us. Matthew 5:7 says, "Blessed are the merciful, for they shall receive mercy." Psalm 18:25 says, "With the merciful you show yourself merciful." On the other hand, it tells us that if we aren't merciful, God will not be merciful to us; and that all our pretenses to faith and a work of conversion will not avail us to obtain mercy, unless we be merciful to them that are in want. Secondly, this very thing is often mentioned in scripture as an essential part of the character of a godly man. Psalm 37:21 says, "The wicked borrows but does not pay back, but the righteous is generous and gives." And again, verse 26, "He is ever lending generously." Psalm 112:5, "It is well with the man who deals generously and lends." And verse 9, "He has distributed freely; he has given to the poor." So, Proverbs 14:31, "Whoever oppresses a poor man insults his Maker, but he who is generous to the needy honors him." Again, Proverbs 21:26 and Isaiah 57:1. A *righteous* man and a *merciful* man are used as synonymous terms: "The *righteous* perish, and *merciful* men are taken away."

It is mentioned in the New Testament as a thing so essential that the contrary cannot consist with a *sincere* love to God. 1 John 3:17–19 says, "But if anyone has the world's goods and sees his brother in need, yet closes his heart against him, how does God's love abide in him? Little children, let us not love in word or talk but in deed and in truth. By this we shall know that we are of the truth and reassure our heart before him." So, the apostle Paul, when he writes to the Corinthians and proposes their contributing for the supply of the poor saints, tells them what he does it for, namely, a trial of their sincerity.

Thirdly, Christ teaches that judgment will be past at the great day according to men's works in this respect. This is taught to us by Christ in the most particular account of the proceedings of that day, that we have in the whole Bible (see Matt. 25:34). It is evident that Christ thus represented the proceedings and determinations of this great day, as turning upon this one point, on purpose and on design, to lead us into this notion and to fix it in us, that a charitable spirit and practice towards our brothers is necessary to salvation.

Gaining Through Giving

Consider what abundant encouragement the word of God gives, that you shall not be losers by your charity and generosity to them who are in want. As there is scarce any duty prescribed in the word of God, which is so much insisted on as this; so there is scarce any to which there are so many promises of reward made. This virtue especially has the promises of this life and that which is to come. If we believe the scriptures, when someone charitably gives to his neighbor in want, the giver has the greatest advantage by it, even greater than the receiver. Acts 20:35 says, "In all things I have shown you that by working hard in this way we must help the weak and remember the words of the Lord Jesus, how he himself said, 'It is more blessed to give than to receive.'" He that gives generously is a happier man than he that receives generously.

Many people are ready to look upon what is given for charitable uses as lost. But we ought not to look upon it as lost, because it benefits those whom we ought to love as ourselves. And not only so, but it is not lost *to us*, if we give any credit to the scriptures. See the advice that *Solomon* gives in Ecclesiastes 11:1, "Cast your bread upon the waters, for you will find it after many days." By casting our bread upon the waters, Solomon means giving it to the poor as appears by the next words, "Give a portion to seven, or even to eight." Waters are sometimes put for people and multitudes.

What strange advice this would seem to many, to cast their bread upon the waters, which would seem to them like throwing it away! What more direct method to lose our bread than to go and throw it into the sea? But the wise man tells us, no, it is not lost; you shall find it again after many days. It is not sunk, but you commit it to providence. You commit it to the winds and waves. However, it will come about to you and you shall find it again after many days. Though it should be many days first, yet you shall find it at last, at a time when you most need it. He that gives to the poor lends to the Lord. And God is not one of those who will not pay again what is lent to him. If you lend anything to God, you commit it into faithful hands. Proverbs 19:17 says, "Whoever is generous to the poor lends to the Lord, and he will repay him for his deed".

A Christian Duty

God will not only pay you again, but he will pay you with great increase.

Do not account that lost that is let out to use. But what is bestowed in charity is lent to the Lord, and he repays with great increase. Isaiah 32:8 says, "But he who is noble plans noble things, and on noble things he stands." Here I would particularly observe,

Firstly, if you give with a spirit of true charity, you shall be rewarded in what is infinitely more valuable than what you give, even eternal riches in heaven. Matthew 10:42 says, "Whoever gives one of these little ones even a cup of cold water because he is a disciple, truly, I say to you, he will by no means lose his reward."

Giving to our needy brothers is in scripture called laying up treasure in heaven in bags that don't age. Jesus says in Luke 12:33, "Sell your possessions, and give to the needy. Provide yourselves with moneybags that do not grow old, with a treasure in the heavens that does not fail, where no thief approaches and no moth destroys." Men, when they have laid their money in their chests, do not suppose that they have thrown it away. But, on the contrary, that it is safe and secure. Much less is treasure thrown away, when it is laid up in heaven. What is laid up there is much safer than what is put in chests or cabinets.

You cannot lay-up treasure on earth, but that it is liable to be stolen or otherwise to fail. But there no thief approaches nor moth corrupts. It is committed to God's care, and he will keep it safely for you. And when you die, you shall receive it with infinite increase. Instead of a part of your earthly substance, you shall receive heavenly riches on which you may live in the greatest fullness, honor, and happiness, to all eternity; and shall never be in want of anything. After feeding with some of your bread those who cannot recompense you, you shall be rewarded at the resurrection and eat bread in the kingdom of God.

Secondly, if you give to the needy in the exercise of moral virtue, you will be in the way greatly to gain by it in your earthly interests. They who give in the exercise of *gracious* charity, are in the way to be gainers both here and hereafter; and those that give in the exercise of a *righteous* generosity and liberality have many temporal promises made to them. We learn by the word of God that they are in the way to be prospered in their outward affairs. Ordinarily such do not lose by it, but such a blessing attends their concerns that they are paid doubly for it. Proverbs 11:24–25 says, "One gives freely, yet grows all the richer; another withholds what he should give, and only suffers want. Whoever brings blessing will be enriched, and one who waters will himself be watered." Proverbs 28:27 states, "Whoever gives to the poor will not want, but he who hides his eyes will get many a curse."

Thirdly, when people give to the needy, they do as it were sowing seed for a crop. When they sow their seed, they might seem to throw it away. Yet they do not look upon it as thrown away because, though they expect not the same again, they expect much more as the fruit of it. And if it be not certain that they shall have a crop, yet they are willing to run the venture of it; for that is the ordinary way wherein men obtain increase. So it is when persons give to the poor. Though the promises of gaining in our outward circumstances perhaps are not absolute; yet it is as much the ordinary consequence of it as increase is by sowing seed. Giving to the poor is in this respect compared to sowing seed, in Ecclesiastes 11:6 "In the morning sow your seed, and at evening withhold not your hand, for you do not know which will prosper, this or that, or whether both alike will be good." By withholding the hand, the wise man means not giving to the poor (see verse 1–2). It intimates, that giving to the poor is as likely a way to obtain prosperity and increase, as sowing seed in a field.

The husbandman doesn't look upon his seed as lost, but is glad that he has opportunity to sow it. It grieves him not that he has land to be sown, but he rejoices in it. For the like reason we should not be grieved that we find needy people to bestow our charity upon. For this is as much an opportunity to obtain increase as the other.

Some may think this is strange doctrine; and it is to be feared that not many will so far believe it as to give to the poor with as much cheerfulness as they sow their ground. However, it is the very doctrine of the word of God.

Fourthly, it is easy for God to make up to men what they give in charity. Few consider how their prosperity or ill success in their outward affairs depends upon providence. There are a thousand turns of providence to which their affairs are liable, whereby God may either add to their outward substance or diminish from it a great deal more than they are ordinarily called to give to their neighbors. How easy is it with God to diminish what they possess by sickness in their families, by drought, or frost, or mildew, or vermin, by unfortunate accidents, by entanglements in their affairs, or disappointments in their business! And how easy is it with God to increase their substance, by suitable seasons, or by health and strength; by giving them fair opportunities for promoting their interest in their dealings with men; by conducting them in his providence, so that they attain their designs; and by innumerable other ways which might be mentioned! How often is it, that only one act of providence in a man's affairs either adds to his estate or diminishes from it more than he would need to give to the poor in a whole year.

Fifthly, God has told us that this is the way to have his blessing attending our affairs. Thus, in the text, Deuteronomy 15:10, "You shall give to him freely, and your heart shall not be grudging when you give to him, because for this the Lord your God will bless you in all your work and in all that you undertake." Proverbs 22:9 says, "Whoever has a bountiful eye will be blessed, for he shares his bread with the poor." It is remarkable how little many men realize the things of religion, whatever they pretend; how little they realize that scripture is the word of God, or if it be, that he speaks true; that notwithstanding all the promises made in scripture to generosity to the poor, yet they are so backward to this duty and are so afraid to trust God with a little of their estates. Observation may confirm the same thing which the word of God teaches on this matter. God, in his providence, generally smiles upon and prospers those men who are of a liberal, charitable and generous spirit.

Sixthly, God has threatened to follow with his curse for those who are uncharitable to the poor; as Proverbs 28:27 says, "Whoever gives to the poor will not want, but he who hides his eyes will get many a curse." It is said, *he who hides his eyes*, because this is the way of uncharitable men. They hide their eyes from seeing the wants of their neighbor. A charitable person, whose heart disposes him to generosity and liberality will be quick sighted to discern the needs of others. They will not be at any difficulty to find out who is in want. They will see objects enough of their charity, let them go whither they will.

But, on the contrary, he that is of an ungenerous spirit, so that it goes against the grain to give anything, he will be always at a loss for objects of his charity. Such men excuse themselves with this, that they don't find anyone to give to. They hide their eyes and will not see their neighbor's wants. If a particular object is presented, they will not very readily see his circumstances. They are a long while in being convinced that he is an object of charity. They hide their eyes. And it is not an easy thing to make them sensitive of the necessities and distresses of their neighbor, or at least to convince them that his necessities are such that they ought to give him any great matter.

Other men, who are of a generous spirit, can very easily see the objects of charity. But the uncharitable are very unapt both to see the proper objects of charity and to see their obligations to this duty. The reason is, that they are of that sort spoken of here by the wise man, *they hide their eyes*. Men will readily see, where they are *willing* to see. But where they hate to see, they will hide their eyes.

God says, such as hides his eyes in this case shall have many a curse. Such a person is on the way to be cursed in soul and body, in both his spiritual and temporal affairs. We have already shown how those that are charitable to the poor are in the way of being blessed. There are so many promises of the divine blessing that we may look upon it as much the way to be blessed in our outward concerns, as sowing seed in a field is the way to have increase. And to be closed and uncharitable is as much the way to be followed with a curse, as to be charitable is the way to be followed with a blessing. To withhold more than is meet tends as much to poverty, as scattering tends to increase (Prov. 11:24). Therefore, if you withhold more than

A Christian Duty

is meet, you will cross your own disposition and will frustrate your own end. What you seek by withholding from your neighbor is your own temporal interest and outward estate. But if you believe the scriptures to be the word of God, you must believe that you cannot take a more direct course to lose, to be crossed and cursed in your temporal interest than this of withholding from your needy neighbor.

Seventhly, consider that you don't know what calamitous and necessitous circumstances you yourselves or your children may be in. Perhaps you are ready to bless yourselves in your hearts, as though there were no danger of you being brought into calamitous and distressing circumstances. There is at present no prospect of it; and you hope you shall be able to provide well for your children. But you little consider what a shifting, changing, uncertain world you live in and how often it has so happened that men have been reduced from the greatest prosperity to the greatest adversity and how often the children of the rich have been reduced to pinching want.

Agreeable to this is the advice that the wise man gives us in Ecclesiastes 11:1–2, "Cast your bread upon the waters, for you will find it after many days. Give a portion to seven, or even to eight, for you know not what disaster may happen on earth." You don't know what calamitous circumstances you may be in yourself in this changeable uncertain world. You don't know what circumstances you or your children may be brought into by captivity, or other unthought-of providences. Providence governs all things. Perhaps you may trust your own wisdom to continue your prosperity. But you cannot alter what God determines and orders in providence, as in the words immediately following the aforementioned text in Ecclesiastes, "If the clouds are full of rain, they empty themselves on the earth, and if a tree falls to the south or to the north, in the place where the tree falls, there it will lie." You cannot alter the determinations of God's providence. You may trust to your own wisdom for future prosperity. But if God have ordained adversity, it *shall come*. As the clouds when full of rain, empty themselves upon the earth, so what is in the womb of providence shall surely come to pass. And as providence casts the tree, whether towards the south, or towards the north, whether for prosperity or adversity, there it shall be for all that you can do to alter it. Agreeably to what the wise man observes in Ecclesiastes 7:13, "Consider the work of God: who can make straight what he has made crooked?"

This consideration, that you don't know what calamity and necessity you may be in yourselves or your children, tends very powerfully to enforce this duty several ways.

This may put you upon considering how your heart would be affected, if it should so be. If it should happen that you or some of your children should be brought into such circumstances as those of your neighbors, how grievous would it be to you! Now perhaps you say of this and the other poor neighbor, that they can do well enough. If they be pinched a little, they can live. Thus, you can make light of their difficulties. But if providence should so order it that you or your children should be brought into the same circumstances, would you make light of them then? Wouldn't you use some other sort of language about it? Wouldn't you think that your case was such as needed the kindness of your neighbors? Wouldn't you think that they ought to be ready to help you? And wouldn't you take it hard if you saw a contrary spirit in them, and saw that they made light of your difficulties?

If one of your children should be brought to poverty by captivity, or otherwise, how would your hearts be affected in such a case? If you should hear that some persons had taken pity on your child and had been very generous to it, would you not think that they did well? Would you be at all apt to accuse them of folly or profuseness, that they should give so much to it?

If ever there should be such a time, your kindness to others now will be but a laying up against such a time. If you yourselves should be brought into calamity and necessity, then would you find what you have given in charity to others, lying ready in store for you. Cast your bread upon the waters, and you shall find it after many days, says the wise man. But when shall we find it? He tells us in the next verse; "Give a portion to seven, or even to eight, for you know not what disaster may happen on earth." Then is the time when you shall find it, when the day of evil comes. You shall again find your bread which you have cast upon the waters when you shall want it most and stand in greatest necessity of it. God will keep it for you against such a time. When other bread shall fail, then God will bring to you the bread which you formerly cast upon the waters so that you shall not starve. He that gives to the poor shall not lack.

Giving to the needy is like laying up against winter, or against a time of calamity. It is the best way of laying up for yourselves and for your children. Children in a time of need very often find their fathers' bread, that bread which their fathers had cast upon the waters. Psalm 37:25 says, "I have been young, and now am old, yet I have not seen the righteous forsaken or his children begging for bread." Why? What is the reason of it? It follows in the next verse, "He is ever lending generously, and his children become a blessing."

Whether the time will ever come or not, that we or our children shall be in distressing want of bread; yet doubtless evil will be on the earth. We shall have our times of calamity, wherein we shall stand in great need of God's pity and help, if not of that of our fellow creatures. And God has promised that at such a time, he that has been of a charitable spirit and practice shall find help.

Such as have been merciful and liberal to others in their

distress, God will not forget it, but will so order it that they shall have help when they are in distress. Yes, their children shall reap the fruit of it in the day of trouble.

God has threatened uncharitable persons that if ever they come to be in calamity and distress they shall be left helpless. Proverbs 21:13 says, "Whoever closes his ear to the cry of the poor will himself call out and not be answered."

"One withholds what he should give...and only suffers want."

PROVERBS 11:24

FOUR

The Objections

I proceed now to answer some objections which are sometimes made against this duty.

The "Not Right Spirit" Objection
I am in a natural condition and if I should give to the poor, I should not do it with a right spirit and so should get nothing by it.

To this I answer we have shown already that a temporal blessing is promised to a righteous generosity and liberality. This is the way to be prospered. This is the way to increase. We find in scripture many promises of temporal blessings to moral virtues; as to diligence in our business, to justice in our dealings, to faithfulness, to temperance.

STEWARDSHIP

So, there are many blessings promised to generosity and liberality.

You may as well make the same objection against any other duty of religion. You may as well object against keeping the sabbath, against prayer, or public worship, or against doing anything at all in religion. For while in a natural condition, you do not do any of these duties with a right spirit. If you say you do these duties because God has commanded or required them of you and you shall sin greatly if you neglect them, you shall increase your guilt and so expose yourselves to the greater damnation and punishment. The same may be said of the neglect of this duty; the neglect of it is as provoking to God.

If you say that you read, pray and attend public worship, because that is the appointed way for you to seek salvation, so is generosity to the poor as much as those. The appointed way for us to seek the favor of God and eternal life is the way of the performance of all known duties, of which giving to the poor is one as much known, and as necessary as reading the scriptures, praying, or any other. Showing mercy to the poor belongs as much to the appointed way of seeking salvation as any other duty. Therefore, this is the way in which Daniel directed Nebuchadnezzar to seek mercy in Daniel 4:27 "Therefore, O king, let my counsel be acceptable to you: break off your sins by practicing righteousness, and your iniquities by *showing mercy to the oppressed*, that there may perhaps be a lengthening of your prosperity."

The "Counting It Righteousness" Objection
If I am liberal and generous, I shall only make a righteousness of it and so it will do me more hurt than good.

To this I say, the same answer may be made to this, as to the former objection, namely, that you may as well make the same objection against doing any religious or moral duty at all. If this be a sufficient objection against deeds of charity, then it is a sufficient objection to prayer. For nothing is more common than for persons to make a righteousness of their prayers. So, it is a good objection against you keeping the Sabbath, or attending any public worship, or ever reading in the Bible. For of all these things you are in danger of making a righteousness. Yes, if the objection be good against doing deeds of charity, then it is as good against doing acts of justice. And you may neglect to speak the truth, you may neglect to pay your debts, you may neglect acts of common humanity; for of all those things you are in danger of making it a righteousness. So that if your objection be good, you may throw out all religion and live like heathens or atheists, and may be thieves, robbers, fornicators, adulterers, murderers, and commit all the sins that you can think of, lest if you should do otherwise, you should make a righteousness of your conduct.

Your objection is that it is not best for you to do as God commands and counsels you to do. We find many commands in scripture to be charitable to the poor. The Bible is full of them; and you are not excepted from those commands. God makes no exception of any particular kinds of persons that are especially in danger of making a righteousness of what they do. And God often directs and counsels persons to this duty. Now will you presume to say that God has not directed you to the best way? He has advised you to do this, but you think it not best for you, that it would do you more hurt than good if you should do it. You think there is other counsel better than God's, and that it is the best way for you to go contrary to God's commands.

The "Not Prospering" Objection
I have in times past given to the poor, but never found myself the better for it. I have heard ministers preach, that giving to the poor was the way to prosper. But I perceive not that I am more prosperous than I was before. Yes, I have met with many misfortunes, crosses, and disappointments in my affairs since. And it may be that some will say, that very year, or soon after the very time, I had been giving to the poor, hoping to be blessed for it, I met with great losses and things went hardly with me; and therefore I do not find what I hear preached about giving to the poor as being the way to be blessed and prosperous, agreeable to my experience.

To this objection I shall answer several things: Perhaps

you looked out for the fulfillment of the promise too soon, before you had fulfilled the condition. As particularly, perhaps you have been so sparing and grudging in your kindness to the poor, that what you have done has been rather a discovery of a covetous, mean spirit, than of any generosity or liberality. The promises are not made to everyone who gives anything at all to the poor, let it be ever so little and after whatsoever manner given. You mistook the promises if you understood them so. A man may give something to the poor and yet be entitled to no promise, either temporal or spiritual. The promises are made to *mercy* and *liberality*. But a man may give something and yet be so mean and grudging in it, that what he gives may be as the apostle calls it, a matter of covetousness. What he does may be more a manifestation of his covetousness and closeness than anything else. But there are no promises made to men's expressing their covetousness.

Perhaps what you gave was not freely given, but as it were of necessity. It was done grudgingly; your hearts were grieved when you gave. And if you gave once or twice what was considerable, yet that does not answer the rule. It may be, for all that, that in the general course of your lives you have been far from being kind and liberal to your neighbors. Perhaps you thought that because you once or twice gave a few shillings to the poor, that then you stood entitled to the promises of being blessed in all your concerns, and of increasing and being established by liberal things, though in general you have lived in a faulty neglect of the duty of charity. You raise objections from experience, before you have tested it. To give once, or twice, or thrice, is not to have trialed, though you give considerably. You cannot make any trial unless you become a generous person, or unless you become such that you may be truly said to be of a liberal and generous practice. Let one who is truly such and has been such in the general course of his life, tell what he has found by experience.

If you have been generous to the poor, and have been met with calamities since, yet how can you tell how much greater calamities and losses you might have been met with if you had been otherwise? You say you have been met with crosses, disappointments and frowns. If you expected to meet with no trouble in the world because you gave to the poor, you mistook the matter. Though there are many and great promises made to the cheerfully generous, yet God has nowhere promised that they shall not find this world a world of trouble. It will be so to all. Man is born to sorrow and must expect no other than to meet with sorrow here. But how can you tell how much greater sorrow you would have been met with if you had been closed and unmerciful to the poor? How can you tell how much greater losses you would have been met with? How much more vexation and trouble would have followed you? Have none ever met with greater frowns in their outward affairs, than you have?

A Christian Duty

How can you tell what blessings God has yet in reserve for you if you do but continue in well-doing? Although God has promised great blessings for charity to the poor, yet he has not limited himself as to the time of the bestowment. If you have not yet seen any evident fruit of your kindness to the poor, yet the time may come when you shall see it remarkably and that at a time when you most stand in need of it. You've cast your bread upon the waters and looked for it, and expected to find it again presently. And sometimes it is so. But this is not promised. It is promised, "you shall find it again *after many days.*" God knows how to choose a time for you, better than you yourselves. You should therefore wait for his time. If you go on in well-doing, God may bring it to you when you stand most in need.

It may be that there is some winter coming, some day of trouble. And God keeps your bread for you against that time. And then God will give you good measure, and pressed down, and shaken together, and running over. We must trust in God's word for the bestowment of the promised reward, whether we can see in what manner it is done or no. Pertinent to the present purpose are those words of the wise man in Ecclesiastes 11:4, "He who observes the wind will not sow, and he who regards the clouds will not reap."

In this context the wise man in speaking of charity to the poor and comparing it to sowing seed; and advises us to trust Providence for success in that, as we do in sowing seed. He that regards the winds and clouds to foretell the prosperity of seed, and will not trust providence with it, is not likely to sow nor to have bread or corn. So, he that will not trust providence for the reward of his charity to the poor is likely to go without the blessing. After the words now quoted, follows his advice, Ecclesiastes 11:6, "In the morning sow your seed, and at evening withhold not your hand, for you do not know which will prosper, this or that, or whether both alike will be good." Therefore, "And let us not grow weary of doing good, for in due season we will reap, if we do not give up" (Gal. 6:9). You think you have not reaped yet. Whether you have or not, go on still in giving and doing good; and if you do so, you shall reap in due time. God only knows the due time, the best time for you to reap.

The "Not Needy Enough" Objection

Some may object against charity to such or such particular persons, that they are not obliged to give them anything for though they be needy, yet they are not in extremity. It is true they meet with difficulty, yet not so but that they can live though they suffer some hardships.

But, it does not answer the rules of Christian charity to relieve those only who are reduced to extremity, as might be abundantly shown. I shall at this time mention but two things as evidence of it.

First, we are commanded to love and treat one another as brothers. 1 Peter 3:8 says, "Finally, all of you, have unity of mind, sympathy, brotherly love, a tender heart, and a humble mind." Now, is it the part of brothers to refuse to help one another, to do anything for each other's comfort and for the relief of each other's difficulties only when they are in extremity? Does it not become brothers and sisters to have a more friendly disposition one towards another than this comes to? And to be ready to be compassionate one to another under difficulties though they be not extreme?

The rule of the gospel is that when we see our brother under any difficulty or burden, we should be ready to bear the burden with him. Galatians 6:2 says, "Bear one another's burdens, and so fulfill the law of Christ." So, we are commanded, "through love serve one another" (Gal. 5:13). The Christian spirit will make us ready to sympathize with our neighbor when we see him under any difficulty. Romans 12:15 says, "Rejoice with those who rejoice, weep with those who weep." When our neighbor is in difficulty, he is afflicted; and we ought to have such a spirit of love to him as to be afflicted with him in his affliction. And if we ought to be afflicted with him, then it will follow that we ought to be ready to relieve him. Because if we are afflicted with him, in relieving him we relieve ourselves. His relief is so far our own relief, as his affliction is our affliction. Christianity teaches us to be afflicted in our neighbor's affliction. And nature teaches us to relieve ourselves when afflicted.

We should behave ourselves one towards another as brothers that are fellow travelers. For we are pilgrims and strangers here on earth and are on a journey. Now, if brothers are on a journey together and one meet with difficulty in the way, does it not fall to the rest to help him, not only in the extremity of broken bones or the like, but as to provision for the journey if his own short fall? It becomes his fellow travelers to afford him a supply out of their stores and not to be over nice, exact, and fearful lest they give him too much: for it is but provision for a journey. And all are supplied when they get to their journey's end.

Second, that we should relieve our neighbor only when in extremity, is not agreeable to the rule of loving our neighbor as ourselves. That rule implies that our love towards our neighbor should work in the same manner, and express itself in the same ways as our love towards ourselves. We are very sensible of our own difficulties. We should also be readily sensible of theirs. From love to ourselves, when we are under difficulties and suffer hardships, we are concerned for our own relief, are quick to seek relief and lay ourselves out for it. And as we would love our neighbor as ourselves, we ought in like manner to be concerned when our neighbor is under difficulty and to seek his relief. We are inclined to be much concerned about our own difficulties, though we be not reduced to extremity and are willing in those cases to lay ourselves out for our own relief. So, as we would love our neighbor as ourselves, we should in like manner sacrifice to obtain relief for him though his difficulties are not extreme.

The "Undeserving" Objection
Some may object against charity to a particular person because he is an ill sort of person. He doesn't deserve that people should be kind to him. He is of a very ill temper, of an ungrateful spirit and particularly, because he has not deserved well of them, but has treated them ill, has been injurious to them and even now entertains an ill spirit against them.

But we are obliged to relieve people in want, notwithstanding these things, both by the general and particular rules of God's word.

Firstly, we are obliged to do so by the *general* rules of scripture. I shall mention two.

Rule 1. That of loving our neighbor as ourselves. A man may be our *neighbor*, though he be an ill sort of man, and even our enemy, as Christ himself teaches us by his discourse with the lawyer (Luke 10:25). A certain lawyer came to Christ, and asked him, what he should do to inherit eternal life? Christ asked him how it was written in the law? He answers, "You shall love the Lord your God with all your heart and with all your soul and with all your strength and with all your mind, and your neighbor as yourself." Christ tells him, that if he shall do thus, he shall live. But then the lawyer asks him, who is his neighbor? Because it was received doctrine among the Pharisees that no man was their neighbor but their friends, and those of the same people and religion. Christ answers him by a parable, or story of a certain man who went down from Jerusalem to Jericho and fell among thieves, who stripped him of his clothes and wounded him, and departed from him, leaving him half dead. Soon after there came a priest that way, who saw the poor man that had been thus cruelly treated by the thieves; but passed by without affording him any relief. The same as done by a Levite. But a certain Samaritan coming that way, as soon as he saw the half-dead man had compassion on him, took him up, bound up his wounds, set him on his own beast, carried him to the inn and took care of him. Paying the innkeeper money for his past and future expense and promising him still more, if he should find it necessary to be at more expense on behalf of the man.

Then Christ asks the lawyer, which of these three, the priest, the Levite, or the Samaritan was neighbor to the man that fell among the thieves. Christ proposed this in such a manner that the lawyer could not help owning that the Samaritan did well in relieving the Jew, that he did the duty of a neighbor to him. Now, there was a deep-rooted enmity between the Jews and the Samaritans. They hated one another more than any other nation in the world. And the Samaritans were a people exceedingly troublesome to the Jews. Yet we see that Christ teaches that the Jews ought to do the part of neighbors to the Samaritans; *i.e.* to love them as themselves. For it was that of which Christ was speaking.

And the consequence was plain. If the Samaritan was neighbor to the distressed Jew, then the Jews by a parity of reason, were neighbors to the Samaritans. If the Samaritan did well in relieving a Jew that was his enemy, then the Jews would do well in relieving the Samaritans their enemies. What I particularly observe is that Christ here plainly teaches that our enemies, those that abuse and injure us, are our neighbors and therefore come under the rule of loving our neighbor as ourselves.

Rule 2. Another general rule that obliges us to the same thing, is where we are commanded to love one another as Christ has loved us. We have it John 13:34, "A new commandment I give to you, that you love one another: just as I have loved you, you also are to love one another." Christ calls it a *new* commandment, with respect to that old commandment of loving our neighbor as ourselves. This command of loving our neighbor as Christ has loved us opens our duty to us in a new manner, and in a further degree than that did. We must not only love our neighbor as ourselves, but as Christ has loved us. We have the same again in John 15:12, "This is my commandment, that you love one another as I have loved you."

Now the meaning of this is not that we should love one another to the same *degree* that Christ loved us, though there ought to be a proportion considering our nature and capacity, but that we should exercise our love one to another in like *manner*. For example, Christ has loved us so as to be willing to deny himself and to suffer greatly in order to help us, so we should be willing to deny ourselves in order to help one another. Christ loved us and showed us great kindness though we were far below him, so should we show kindness to those of our fellow men who are far below us. Christ denied himself to help us though we are not able to recompense him, so should we be willing to lay out ourselves to help our neighbor freely expecting nothing in return. Christ loved us, was kind to us and was willing to relieve us, though we were very evil and hateful, of an evil disposition, not deserving any good, but deserving only to be hated and treated with indignation; so we should be willing to be kind to those who are of an ill disposition and are very undeserving. Christ loved us and laid himself out to relieve us, though we were his enemies and had treated him ill. So we, as we would love one another as Christ has loved us, should relieve those who are our enemies, those who hate us, have an ill spirit toward us and have treated us ill.

Secondly, we are obliged to this duty by many *particular* rules. We are particularly required to be kind to the unthankful and to the evil. And therein to follow the example of our heavenly Father who causes his sun to rise on the evil and on the good, and sends rain on the just and on the unjust. We are obliged not only to be kind to them that are so to us, but to them that hate and that despitefully use us. I don't need to mention the particular places which speak to the effect.

When persons are virtuous, pious, of a grateful disposition and are friendly disposed towards us, they are more the objects of our charity for it and our obligation to kindness to them is the greater. Yet if things are otherwise, that does not render them unfit objects of our charity nor set us free from obligation to kindness towards them.

The "I Can't Afford It" Objection
Some may object from their own circumstances that they have nothing to spare; they don't have enough for themselves.

I answer, it must doubtless be allowed that in some cases, people, by reason of their own circumstances are not obliged to give to others. For instance, if there's a contribution for the poor, they are not obliged to join in the contribution who are in as much need as those are for whom the contribution is made. It smacks of ridiculous vanity in them to contribute with others for such as are not more needy than they. It smacks of a proud desire to conceal their own circumstances and pretentious to have them account to what they in truth are.

There are scarcely any who don't make this objection as they interpret it. There is no person who won't say that he has not more than enough for himself as he may mean by *enough*. He may intend that he has not more than he desires or more than he can dispose of to his own advantage; or not so much, but that if he had anything less, he should look upon himself in worse circumstances than he is in now. He will own, that he could live if he had less. But then he will say he could not live so well. Rich men may say they have not more than enough for themselves, as they may mean by it. They need it all they may say, to support their honor and dignity as is proper for the place and degree in which they stand. Those who are poor will say *they* have not too much for themselves. Those who are of the middle sort will say, *they* have not too much for themselves. And the rich will say, *they* have not too much for themselves. Therefore, none will be found to give to the poor!

In many cases, we may by the rules of the gospel, be obliged to give to others when we cannot do it without suffering ourselves. As if our neighbor's difficulties and necessities are much greater than our own and we see that he is not like to be otherwise relieved, we should be willing to suffer with him and to take part of his burden on ourselves. Else, how is that rule of *bearing one another's burdens* fulfilled? If we are never obliged to relieve others' burdens, but when we can do it without burdening ourselves, then how do we bear our neighbor's burdens when we bear no burden at all? Though we may not have an excess, we might be obliged to afford relief to others who are in much greater necessity. As shown by that rule in Luke 3:11, "Whoever has two tunics is to share with him who has none, and whoever has food is to do likewise." Yes, they who are very poor may be obliged to give for the relief of others in much greater distress than they. If there's no other way of relief, those who have the lightest burden are still obliged to take some part of their neighbor's burden making it the more bearable. A brother may be obliged to help a brother in extremity, though they are both very much in want. The apostle commends the Macedonian Christians, that they were generous to their brothers though they themselves were in deep poverty.

Those who have not too much for themselves are willing to spare seed to sow, that they may have fruit hereafter. Perhaps they need that which they scatter in the field and seem to throw away. They may need it for bread for their families. Yet they will spare seed to sow, that they may provide for the future and may have increase. But we have already shown that giving to the poor is in scripture compared to sowing seed and is as much the way to increase as the sowing of seed is. It does not tend to poverty, but the contrary. It is not the way to diminish our substance, but to increase it. All the difficulty in this matter is in trusting God with what we give, in trusting his promises. If men

The "Uncertainty" Objection

Some may object concerning a particular person, that they don't know with certainty whether he is an object of charity or not. They are not perfectly acquainted with his circumstances. Neither do they know what sort of man he is. They don't know whether he's truly in want. Or if they know this, they don't know how he came to be in want, whether it was not by his own idleness, or prodigality. Thus, they argue that they cannot be obliged until they know these things with certainty.

I reply,

Firstly, this is Nabal's objection for which he is greatly condemned in Scripture (see 1 Sam. 25). David in exile, came and begged relief of Nabal. Nabal objected, 1 Samuel 25:10–11, "Who is David? Who is the son of Jesse? There are many servants these days who are breaking away from their masters. Shall I take my bread and my water and my meat that I have killed for my shearers and give it to men who come from I do not know where?" His objection was, that David was a stranger to him. He did not know who he was, nor what his circumstances were. All he knew was that he was a runaway, and he was not obliged to support and harbor a runaway. He objected, that he didn't know that he was a proper object of charity; he didn't know but he was very much the contrary.

But Abigail in no way tolerated his behavior but greatly condemned it. She calls him a man of Belial and says that he was as his name was. Nabal was his name, and folly was with him. And her behavior was very contrary to his and she is greatly commended for it. The Holy Spirit tells us in that chapter (1 Sam. 25:3) that she was a woman of discernment. At the same time God exceedingly frowned on Nabal's behavior on this occasion, as we are informed in verse 38 that about ten days after God smote Nabal, he died.

This story is doubtless told to us partly for this end, to disapprove of too great a scrupulosity as to the objection on whom we bestow our charity. This is merely an objection against charity to others, because we do not certainly know their circumstances. It is true, when we have opportunity to be certainly acquainted with their circumstances, it is good to embrace it. And to be influenced in a measure by probability in such cases, is not to be condemned. Yet it is better to give to several that are not objects of charity, than to send away empty one that is.

Secondly, we are commanded to be kind to strangers whom we know not, nor their circumstances. This is commanded in many places, but I shall mention only one. Hebrews 13:2 states, "Do not neglect to show hospitality to strangers, for thereby some have entertained angels unawares." By strangers here the apostle means one whom we don't know, and whose circumstances we don't know; as is evident by these words, "for thereby some have entertained angels unawares." Those who entertained angels unawares did not know the persons whom they entertained, nor their circumstances. Else how could it be unawares?

The "Not Been Asked" Objection

Some may say that they are not obliged to give to the poor until they are asked. If anyone is in need, let him come and make known to me and then it will be the time for me to give. Or if he needs a church contribution, let him come and ask. I do not know that the congregation or church is obliged to relieve until they ask for relief.

I answer, it is surely the most charitable to relieve the needy in a way where we do them the greatest kindness. Now it is certain that we shall do them a greater kindness by inquiring into their circumstances and relieving them without making them beg. None of us who, if it were the case, would look upon it kindlier than for our neighbors to inquire into our circumstances and help us of their own accord. To have our neighbors begging in order to obtain relief is painful. It is more charitable, more brotherly, more becoming of Christians and disciples of Jesus to do it without them having to ask. I think this is self-evident, and so needs no proof.

This is not agreeable to the character of the noble man

A Christian Duty

given in scripture; namely, that he devises noble things (Isa. 32:8). It is not to devise noble things, if we neglect all charity till the poor come begging. But to inquire who stands in need of our charity, and to plan to relieve them in the way that shall do them the greatest kindness; that is to devise noble things.

We would not commend a man for doing so to his own brother. If a man had his own brother or sister in great straits and he were well able to supply them, under the pretense that if he or she want anything let them come and ask and I will give them. We should hardly think such a man behaved like a brother. Christians are commanded to love as brothers, to look upon one another as brothers in Christ and to treat one another as such.

We should commend others for taking a method contrary to that which is proposed by the objector. If we should hear or read of people who were so charitable, who took such care of the poor and were so concerned that none among them should suffer, who were proper objects of charity; that they were given to diligently inquire into the circumstances of their neighbors to find out who were needy, and liberally supplied them of their own accord; I say, if we should hear or read of such people, would it not appear well to us? Would we not think better of those people on that account?

The "Own Fault" Objection
He has brought himself to want by his own fault.

In reply, it must be considered what you mean by his fault. If you mean he lacks a natural faculty to manage affairs to his advantage, that is to be considered as his calamity. Such a faculty is a gift that God bestows on some, and not on others. And it is not owing to themselves. You ought to be thankful that God has given you such a gift, which he has denied the person in question. And it will be a very suitable way for you to show your thankfulness, to help those to whom that gift is denied and let them share the benefit of it with you. This is as reasonable as that he to whom providence has imparted sight should be willing to help him to whom sight is denied, and that he should have the benefit of the sight of others who has none of his own. Or, as that he to whom God has given wisdom should be willing that the ignorant should have the benefit of his knowledge.

If they have been reduced to want by some oversight and are to be blamed that they did not consider for themselves better, yet that does not free us from all obligation to charity towards them. If we should forever refuse to help men because of that, it would be for us to make their inconsiderateness and imprudent act an unpardonable crime. Quite contrary to the rules of the gospel which insist so much upon forgiveness. We should not be disposed so highly to resent such an oversight in any for whom we have a dear affection, as our children or our friends. We should not refuse to help them in that need and distress, which they brought upon themselves by their own inconsiderateness. But we ought to have a dear affection and concern for the welfare of all our fellow Christians, whom we should love as brothers as Christ has loved us.

If they come to want by idleness and prodigality, yet we are not thereby excused from all obligation to relieve them unless they continue in those vices. If they continue not in those vices, the rules of the gospel direct us to forgive them. And if their fault be forgiven then it will not remain to be a bar in the way of our charitably relieving them. If we do otherwise, we shall act in a manner very contrary to the rule of *loving one another as Christ has loved us*. Now Christ has loved us, pitied us, and greatly put himself out, to relieve us from that want and misery which we brought on ourselves by our own folly and wickedness. We foolishly and perversely threw away those riches with which we were provided, upon which we might have lived and been happy to all eternity.

If they continue in the same ways still, yet that doesn't excuse us from charity to their families that are innocent. If we cannot relieve those of their families without their having something of it, yet that ought not to be a bar in the way of our charity. And that because it is supposed that those of their families are proper objects of charity. And those that are so, we are bound to relieve. The command is positive and absolute. If we look upon that which the heads of the families have of what we give, to be entirely lost; yet we had better lose something of our estate than suffer those who are really proper objects of charity to remain without relief.

The "Someone Else's Problem" Objection
Some may object and say others don't do their duty. If others did their duty, the poor would be sufficiently supplied. If others did as much as we in proportion to their ability and obligation, the poor would have enough to help them out of their need. Or some may say it belongs to others more than it does to us. They have relations that ought to help them. Or there are others to whom it more properly belongs than to us.

In reply, we ought to relieve those who are in want though brought to it through others' fault. If our neighbor is poor, though others are to blame that it is so, yet that doesn't excuse us from helping him. If it belongs to others more than to us, yet if those others will neglect their duty and our neighbor therefore remains in want, we may be obliged to relieve him. If a man be brought into dire straits through the injustice of others, suppose by thieves or robbers as the poor Jew whom the Samaritan relieved; yet we may be obliged to relieve him, though it be not through our fault that he is in want but through that of other men. And whether that fault is a commission or a neglect, doesn't alter the case.

As to the poor Jew that fell among thieves between Jerusalem and Jericho, it more properly belonged to those thieves who brought him into that distress to relieve him than to any other person. Yet seeing they would not do it; others were not excused. And the Samaritan did no more than his duty, relieving him as he did though it properly belonged to others. Thus, if a man has children or other relations to whom it most properly belongs to relieve him, yet if they will not do it, the obligation to relieve him falls upon others. So, for the same reason we should do the more for the relief of the poor, because others neglect to do their proportion or what belongs to them. And that because by the neglect of others to do their proportion they need the more, their necessity is the greater.

The "State will Provide" Objection
The law makes provision for the poor and obliges the respective towns in which they live to provide for them. Therefore, some argue that there is no occasion for particular persons to exercise any charity this way. They say the case is not the same with us now as it was in the primitive church for Christians were under a heathen government. And, however the charity of Christians in those times is much to be commended, yet now, by reason of our different circumstances there is no occasion for private charity. Because, in the state in which Christians now are, provision is made for the poor.

This objection is built upon these two suppositions, both which I suppose are false.

Firstly, that the towns are obliged by law to relieve everyone who otherwise would be an object of charity. This I suppose to be false unless it is supposed that none are proper objects of charity but those that have no estate left to live upon, which is very unreasonable and what I have already shown to be false, in answer to the fourth objection in showing that it does not answer the rules of Christian charity to relieve only those who are reduced to extremity.

Nor do I suppose it was ever the design of the law, requiring the various towns to support their own poor to cut off all occasion for Christian charity. Nor is it fit that there should be such a law. It is fit that the law should make provision for those that have no estates of their own. It is not fit that persons who are reduced to that extremity should be left to so precarious a source of supply as a voluntary charity. They are in extreme need of relief and therefore it is fit that there should be something sure for them to depend on. But voluntary charity in this corrupt world is an uncertain thing. Therefore, the wisdom of the legislature did not think fit to leave those who are so reduced upon such a precarious foundation for subsistence. But I don't suppose that it was ever the design of the law to make such provision for all that are in want as to leave no room for Christian charity.

A Christian Duty

Secondly, this objection is built upon another supposition which is equally false, namely, that there are in fact none who are proper objects of charity but those that are relieved by the town. Let the design of the law be what it will, yet if there are in fact persons who are so in want as to stand in need of our charity, then that law does not free us from obligation to relieve them by our charity. For as we have just now shown in answer to the last objection, if it more properly belongs to others to relieve them than us; yet if they don't do it, we are not free. So that if it's true that it *belongs* to the town to relieve all who are proper objects of charity; yet if the town *in fact* doesn't do it, we are not excused.

If one of our neighbors suffers through the fault of a particular person, a thief or robber, or of a town, it doesn't alter the case. But if he suffers and be without relief, it is an act of Christian charity for us to relieve him. Now it is too obvious to be denied that there are in fact people so in want that it would be a charitable act for us to help them, notwithstanding all that is done by the town.

A man must hide his mental eyes to think otherwise.

Classics of
Biblical Spirituality

H&E

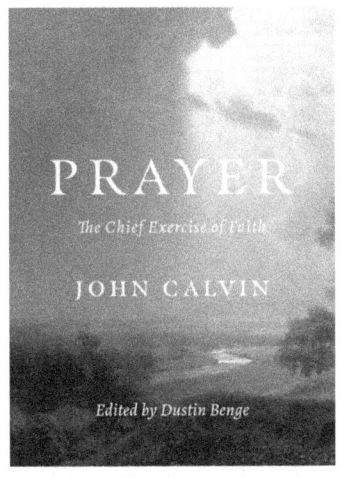

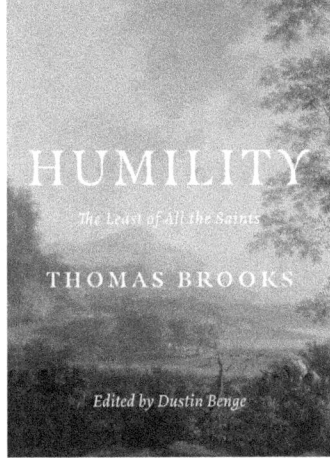

Other books in the series available at hesedandemet.com

www.ingramcontent.com/pod-product-compliance
Lightning Source LLC
Chambersburg PA
CBHW072208100526
44589CB00015B/2421